Awesome Inventions You Use Every Day

MARVELOUS MEDICAL INVENTIONS

RYAN JACOBSON

LERNER PUBLICATIONS COMPANY
MINNEAPOLIS

Lerner Publications Company
A division of Lerner Publishing Group, Inc.
241 First Avenue North
Minneapolis, MN 55401 U.S.A.

Website address: www.lernerbooks.com

Library of Congress Cataloging-in-Publication Data

Jacobson, Ryan.
Marvelous medical inventions /
by Ryan Jacobson.
p.   cm. — (Awesome inventions you use
every day)
Includes index.
ISBN 978–1–4677–1095–4 (lib. bdg. : alk. paper)
ISBN 978–1–4677–1684–0 (eBook)
1. Medicine—History—Juvenile literature. 2. Medical
innovations—History—Juvenile literature. 3. Medical
technology—Juvenile literature. I. Title.
R133.5.J33 2014
610—dc23   2012041776

Manufactured in the United States of America
1 – PP – 7/15/13

CONTENTS

INTRODUCTION

FEEL-GOOD MEDICAL INVENTIONS

Getting sick is no fun. Well, maybe staying home from school isn't so bad. But getting really sick is a bummer. Lucky for us, we have doctors. Luckier yet, doctors have all sorts of technology to help us get well. But have you ever wondered, "What if those helpful tools were never invented?"

Imagine going to the doctor and being told to eat a mouse. Or to treat your cut with moldy bread. A few hundred years ago, either might have happened. Some doctors would even guess what was wrong with you by tasting your pee!

Yes, we're lucky all right. Doctors and scientists have taken big steps over the past centuries. The average person lives forty years longer than people did two hundred years ago. You know what that means? Forty extra years of eating pizza! Get ready to take a look at twelve awesome inventions. You'll find out why you wouldn't want to live without them.

In earlier times, cures were sometimes grosser than diseases. Some healers used mice or moldy bread.

X-RAY

You slip. You fall. A sharp pain shoots from your ankle. What's a person to do? Blame your sister, of course. But after that, it's time for a trip to the doctor. And thanks to an accident that happened more than a hundred years ago, your doctor will tell you what's busted.

In 1895 a German scientist named Wilhelm Röntgen was doing an experiment with radiation. Radiation is a form of energy, such as light or heat. Röntgen was studying what happens when electricity passes through a gas. He shot cathode rays out of a heated tube. These rays are made from tiny particles called electrons.

Everything was going fine until Röntgen noticed that a nearby screen was glowing. Impossible! Röntgen knew that electrons from the cathode rays could not be causing the screen to glow. The situation was weird. It got downright scary. Röntgen put his hand in front of the glowing screen and saw through the hand to his bones. Eek!

Röntgen was no dummy. He figured out that another kind of radiation must be coming from the tube. He called his discovery X-rays. Less than three months later, the first X-ray of a broken bone was taken.

X-rays allow doctors to take pictures of your bones. These rays are made up of particles called photons. Bones absorb photons. So when X-rays are aimed at you, electrons go through you. But many of the photons stick to your bones. X-ray machines take pictures of the photons. The result is an image of your bones—cracks, breaks, and all.

Don't worry. Getting an X-ray doesn't hurt. It doesn't feel like anything. That sure beats life before X-rays. A doctor would poke and pinch your broken ankle. Then he would guess what the problem was. If he guessed wrong, you might never walk right again!

Wilhelm Röntgen of Germany discovered x-rays.

x-rays allow us to see images of the human skeleton.

CONTACT LENS

Glasses help people to see well. Contact lenses are the supersecret version of glasses. Some of your classmates probably wear contact lenses. You might not even know it.

People first used tools to see better almost two thousand years ago. (That's so far back, even your teacher wasn't born yet!) Around A.D. 100, the people of Rome, in modern Italy, learned that light bends when it passes through glass. They soon discovered that curved glass bends light even more. Let's say the glass bends away from your eyes. Things seen through the glass will look bigger. If the glass bends toward your eyes, things will look smaller.

Throughout history, scientists put this knowledge to good use. From magnifying glasses to eyeglasses, people used lenses (curved glass) to boost their vision. In 1508 an inventor named Leonardo da Vinci had a crazy thought. He wondered, "What if tiny lenses could be put on people's eyes?" Cool idea. But it didn't happen for almost four hundred years!

Then, in 1887, F. A. Müller of Germany came to the rescue. Müller created the first contact lenses. The good news: They were small enough to fit on a person's eyes. The bad news: they were made out of glass. It really hurt to wear them for long.

In modern times, most contact lenses are formed from soft plastic. These lenses can be worn all day without any problems. Color contacts even make a person's eyes seem to be a different color!

PAIN MEDICINE

You're playing a basketball game on your driveway. Suddenly your head starts to hurt, and you start to miss your shots. But it's okay! You run inside and tell your mom, and she feeds you a pill or two. Before long, you're back in the game.

Yep, pain medicine is pretty cool stuff. Not feeling pain is way better than feeling pain. People have been taking pain medicine since 3000 B.C. Ancient Egyptians used a powder made of willow bark. This cure was a natural form of aspirin. (Aspirin is a chemical that relieves pain and fever.) But willow bark wasn't perfect. It tasted worse than your dog's jerky treats. And it caused stomachaches and vomiting.

For much of history, the big question was which is worse: pain or puking? If you said both, you're right. Doctors tried other types of pain medicine. Patients were given drugs such as heroin, morphine, and opium. But those drugs were often deadly.

Barfing is better than dying. Scientists started thinking, "Maybe willow bark isn't so bad." And hey, they were scientists. They must have been able to keep the painkiller part and get rid of the puking part. Right?

Nope. Geniuses around the world tried to solve the problem, but no one could. Until 1897, that is. German scientist Felix Hoffmann found the perfect mix of chemicals. Modern aspirin was born. It only took forty-nine hundred or so years. Not bad.

THE GERMAN COMPANY BAYER was the first to sell aspirin. But during World War I (1914–1918), Germany and the United States were enemies. The United States and its allies could not get aspirin. Anyone who was able to re-create the aspirin formula stood to make big money. An Australian man named George Nicholas borrowed kitchen tools from his wife. With a little hard work, he remade aspirin. The pain medicine was available again!

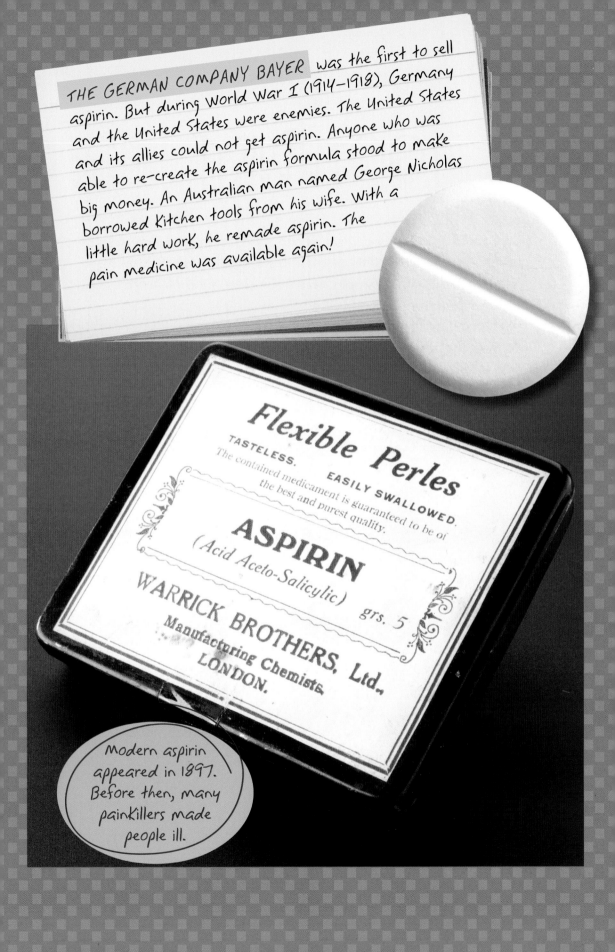

Flexible Perles

TASTELESS. EASILY SWALLOWED.

The contained medicament is guaranteed to be of the best and purest quality.

ASPIRIN

(Acid Aceto-Salicylic)

grs. 5

WARRICK BROTHERS, Ltd.,
Manufacturing Chemists,
LONDON.

Modern aspirin appeared in 1897. Before then, many painkillers made people ill.

TOOTHPASTE

You use toothpaste every day. Hopefully the person next to you does too. Otherwise, gross. Toothpaste doesn't just fight bad breath, though. It also cleans and strengthens teeth. That's a big deal. So big that people have been cleaning their teeth for more than six thousand years.

The coolest thing about toothpaste isn't the taste. It's not how clean it makes your mouth feel either. No, the best thing is that you don't have to use what people used before toothpaste!

Ancient Egyptians mixed mint leaves and dried flowers. Okay, that could have been worse. The Chinese blended twigs and flower pedals with crushed bones. Now that's a little yucky. But get this: the Romans used a tooth-cleaning mixture with pee as an ingredient! You'd almost rather have a cavity, wouldn't you?

Luckily, someone invented toothpaste. Who? Um, no one really knows. But in 1873, Colgate became the first company to sell toothpaste. You can check the label. The ingredient list is pee-free.

Modern toothpaste is a blend of chemicals such as fluoride, detergents, and abrasives. Each part plays a special role. Fluoride strengthens teeth. Detergents loosen the gunk stuck to teeth. Abrasives clean all of that gunk away. Most modern toothpastes include minty flavoring too. With those ingredients working together, no one will ever know that you ate a tuna, garlic, and onion sandwich for lunch.

Toothpaste includes a blend of chemicals that work together to clean teeth.

Colgate TOOTH POWDER

THE TOOTHBRUSH HAS ITS OWN HISTORY. It starts around 3000 B.C., with chew sticks. The first bristle toothbrush appeared in 1498. The bristles were made out of pig hair! Nylon bristles appeared in 1938. During World War II (1939–1945), soldiers made tooth care very popular. During the war, the military made them brush their teeth every day. Later, soldiers brought those habits home to their families.

SYRINGE

Unless you're crazy, you probably don't like shots. And why would you? Shots hurt! But they are important. Shots help to prevent diseases such as polio, the flu, and chicken pox. They can even save a person's life.

To give shots, doctors use a syringe. This tool is as brilliant as it is simple. A syringe is basically just a tube with a needle on one end and a plunger on the other. No, the plunger's not like the one from your bathroom. But it works the same way. When a syringe's plunger gets pushed down, it forces medicine out of the tube. When the plunger gets pulled, it creates suction inside the tube.

The needle of a syringe is hollow inside with a tiny hole at its tip. If that needle gets poked into your arm, guess what happens when the plunger is pulled. Yep, the suction pulls blood out of your body and into the tube. The poke hurts a little, but it's pretty cool to see. If there's medicine in the tube and the plunger gets pushed down, that medicine goes into your body.

Just who invented this wonderful piece of equipment? Dominique Anel was a surgeon in the late 1600s and the early 1700s. He worked in the army of King Louis XIV of France. Anel's job was to clean soldiers' wounds. But blood kept getting in the way. To fix the problem, Anel invented the modern syringe. He used it to clean wounds with suction. So next time a doctor gives you a shot, don't blame the doctor. Blame Dominique Anel!

The syringe has many uses, from cleaning wounds to delivering medicine.

BAND-AID

Who doesn't love Band-Aids? There's something cool about wearing one. It's like telling the world, "I have a tiny cut, and I'm not afraid to show it!" Yes, Band-Aids are part of growing up. But have you ever wondered how they came to be?

Josephine Dickson was a devoted wife. She was also quite clumsy. She caused some sort of minor accident almost every day—usually cutting a finger or burning one in the kitchen. Each night, her husband Earle came home from work. And each night, Earle bandaged his wife's scratch of the day with cotton and tape.

Earle started to think, "There has to be a better way!" He began planning ahead. He would take a long piece of tape and stick squares of cotton to it, all in a row. Then, when his wife needed a bandage, it was already made for her.

This trick worked so well that Earle started seeing dollar signs. He told his bosses at a company called Johnson & Johnson. They loved the idea so much that they gave him a better job and more money. In 1920 Johnson & Johnson began selling premade bandages, or Band-Aids. But nobody wanted them. Earle's idea was a dud! So the company said, "What should we do with these Band-Aids that no one's buying?"

Somebody answered, "Oh, just give them to the Boy Scouts."

And that's what Johnson & Johnson did. All at once, moms and dads everywhere fell in love with Band-Aids. The bandages soon became the best cure for a common boo-boo. Well, second best. You still can't beat a mom's kiss.

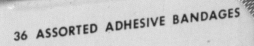

LASER SURGERY

When you think of lasers, you probably imagine sci-fi movies. But lasers are real. They're not even new.

A laser beam is a form of light. Normally, light shines in every direction. Light also gets dimmer as it travels farther from its source. But laser beams do not.

Lasers cause tiny particles called atoms to release their energy (light) in one direction. That burst of energy causes more atoms to release their energy. That causes even more atoms to release their energy. The result is a straight beam of light. The beam can shine for a very long way. Scientists have even sent laser beams all the way to the moon!

What does this have to do with doctors? Well, if you've ever been outside on a summer day, you know that light gives off energy as heat. Lasers do too. Doctors can put that heat to good use. For one thing, the heat can cut or remove human tissue!

Believe it or not, the idea of lasers has been around since 1916. Several inventors tried to build lasers, but nobody could get one to work. Theodore Harold Maiman created the first working laser in 1960. Most people were like, "So what? It's useless!" But a few saw the potential.

In 1987 Dr. Stephen Trokel found that cutting thin layers of tissue off the surface of the eye could improve vision. Yikes! Would you volunteer to be his first patient? No need to worry. A laser made the tricky cuts with ease. The surgery worked! Since then, laser eye surgery has become common. The process is not as cool as a laser sword, but it's still pretty cool.

A laser beam is a form of light that travels in one direction.

Dr. Theodore Maiman built the world's first working laser.

BRACES

Ah, braces—those metal attachments that cover your teeth. They make your mouth look like it's part robot. But the extra weight on your pearly whites is totally worth it to scare younger brothers and sisters with your metal chompers. You'll have a beautiful smile for the rest of your life too.

People wear braces to straighten their teeth. Braces push teeth from where they are to where they're supposed to be. Unfortunately, that pushing can't happen all at once. What if someone pushed you really hard? You'd fall over. But if someone pushed you a little bit at a time, you'd get to where you were supposed to be.

Braces are like that too. Instead of pushing all at once, braces push teeth a small distance and hold them until the teeth stay put on their own. Then an orthodontist adjusts the braces to push the teeth a little more. Sooner or later, the teeth end up in the right place. Sometimes the process takes years. Then it's bye-bye, braces. Hooray!

Braces can be uncomfortable, like visiting your weird aunt. But modern braces feel like a soft blanket compared to history's first braces. The people of ancient Greece tried out braces around 1000 B.c. They wrapped metal bands around each tooth, one at a time. Ouch!

Many inventors throughout history tried to fix crooked smiles. In 1728 French dentist Pierre Fauchard came along. He was a brilliant thinker with all sorts of ideas about teeth. He even wrote a book called *The Surgeon Dentist.* His horseshoe-shaped bandeau became the model for modern braces. The bandeau was tied onto the mouth with wires. It stretched the arch of the mouth, which created a space for teeth to straighten out. So the next time you're chasing your brothers and sisters with your metal chompers, say a small thanks to Dr. Fauchard.

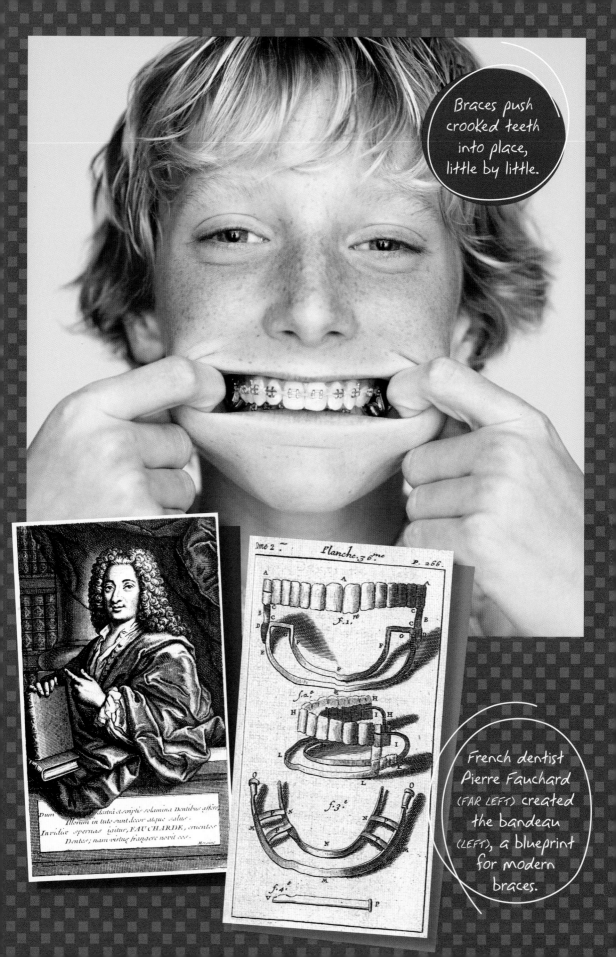

Braces push crooked teeth into place, little by little.

French dentist Pierre Fauchard (FAR LEFT) created the bandeau (LEFT), a blueprint for modern braces.

THERMOMETER

Tell the truth. You've faked being sick to stay home from school. Too bad your parents have a lie detector: a thermometer!

Doctors and moms use thermometers to find out your body's temperature. Thermometers let them know if your body is okay, sick, or really sick! A normal body temperature is 98.6°F (37°C). The farther your temperature is from that number, the sicker you probably are.

The coolest thing about thermometers is that anyone can make them. Plenty of people have. Thermometers work because liquids fill more space or less space as their temperature changes. Cold liquid takes up more space than hot liquid. You already know this if you've ever left a soda in the freezer. The can explodes. Why? Because the liquid becomes too big for the can!

History's most famous thermometer maker was Gabriel Fahrenheit. In 1724 he put the chemical mercury in a tube. He set 32°F (0°C) as water's freezing temperature. He also set 212°F (100°C) as water's boiling temperature. Then he marked 180 degrees in between those points. People in modern times still use this type of thermometer.

Many modern thermometers are electronic—no liquid involved.

WITH HELP FROM A PARENT OR A TEACHER, you can build your own thermometer. Begin by mixing together 3 ounces (90 milliliters) of water and 3 ounces of rubbing alcohol in a glass. Add 2 drops of food coloring. (Don't drink your mixture!) Pour the mix into a clear, empty water bottle until the bottle is one-quarter full. Place a clear straw into the mixture. The end of the straw should be near the bottom of the bottle but shouldn't touch it. Wrap clay or Play-Doh around the top of the bottle. This should seal the straw in place. Water will go up and down in the straw as the temperature changes!

ANESTHESIA

Surgery is a scary word. No one wants to be cut open and have his or her insides messed with. Lucky for us, there's anesthesia. This blend of chemicals puts patients to sleep.

How much scarier was surgery two hundred years ago? Back then, doctors didn't have anesthesia. They used deadly drugs such as opium. Or they gave patients alcohol to drink. Alcohol numbed the pain a little, but patients could still feel what their doctors were doing. Sometimes, doctors even knocked out their patients by whacking them on the head!

That all changed in 1846. Dr. William Morton was about to fix a patient's jaw. Before he started, the doctor decided to use a chemical called ether to put his patient to sleep. Other doctors were shocked when the patient woke with no memory of the surgery. Some doctors even thought the patient was lying!

Morton's use of ether inspired the creation of anesthesia. Modern anesthesia blends all sorts of chemicals into a gas that patients breathe. The chemicals affect the spinal cord to keep your body from moving. They affect a part of the brain called the brain stem, which puts you to sleep. And they affect another part of the brain, the cerebral cortex, so you don't feel any pain.

That sure beats getting smacked in the head.

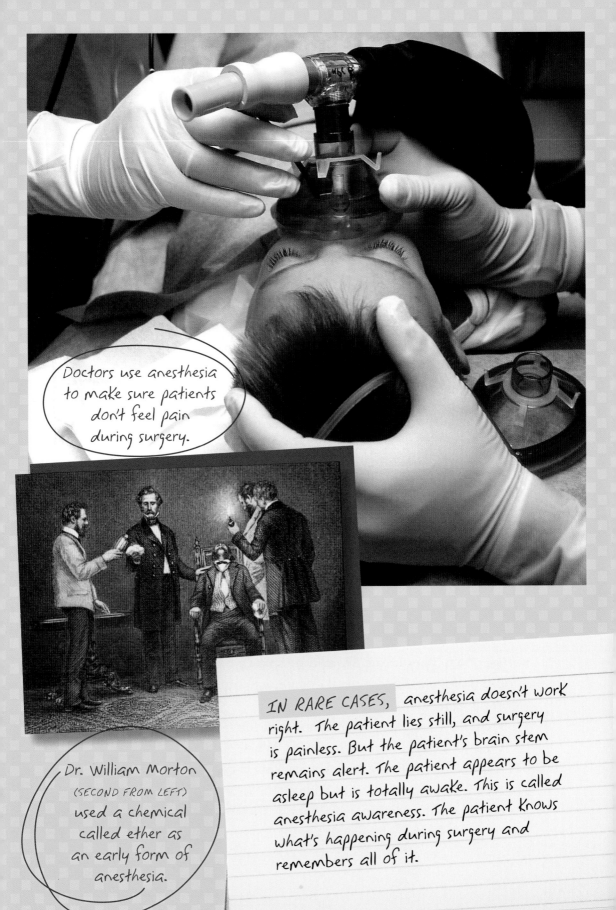

Doctors use anesthesia to make sure patients don't feel pain during surgery.

Dr. William Morton (SECOND FROM LEFT) used a chemical called ether as an early form of anesthesia.

IN RARE CASES, anesthesia doesn't work right. The patient lies still, and surgery is painless. But the patient's brain stem remains alert. The patient appears to be asleep but is totally awake. This is called anesthesia awareness. The patient knows what's happening during surgery and remembers all of it.

WHEELCHAIRS

At some point in history, somebody must have said, "I'm sick of standing. I'm going to sit." And the chair was invented. That has to be the best invention ever—except maybe video games. The wheel is near the top of the list too. So what could be more awesome than putting the chair and the wheel together?

Wheelchairs help sick or disabled people move around. Before wheelchairs, the ancient Greeks used wheeled beds as early as 530 B.C. A few hundred years later, the Chinese put people in wheelbarrows to move them. The earliest wheelchairs appeared in China around A.D. 525. They looked like benches on three wheels.

By the 1500s, some royals in Europe were using wheelchairs—even though they didn't need to. A fancy wheelchair with footrests was made for King Phillip II of Spain.

One of history's most famous wheelchairs was the Bath Chair. (Don't let the name fool you. It wasn't a moving bathtub.) It came from Bath, England. John Dawson created the chair in 1783. He placed two large wheels in back and one small wheel in front. Wealthy (and often healthy) people used these wheelchairs to roll around town in comfort. The Bath Chair was the world's most popular wheelchair for much of the nineteenth century.

By 1900 many wheelchairs looked like tricycles. Pedals on the chairs' handlebars allowed people to move without using their legs. In 1912 a small engine was added to make the world's first motorized wheelchair.

Modern wheelchairs have come ever further. Of course, most modern chairs have four wheels. Wheelchairs are light and can fold to fit inside cars. Some allow disabled people to play wheelchair sports such as basketball. Sport wheelchairs are smaller, lighter, and built for speed. They're the race cars of the wheelchair world!

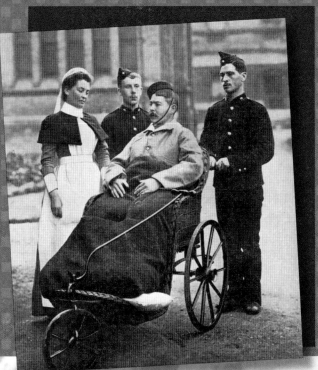

Wheelchairs of the past, such as this chair from England in 1896, had different designs than modern wheelchairs.

Sport wheelchairs are made for people on the go.

PROSTHETIC LIMBS

Ever dreamed of being a pirate? Have you pretended to wear a hook for a hand? Or maybe a peg for a leg? If so, then you know what an artificial (false) limb is.

The oldest artificial body part ever found came from Egypt. Experts dated the part to around 1000 B.C. It was a toe made of wood and leather. (Someone must have stubbed his toe really hard to need a wooden one!) The design worked well. In fact, artificial body parts stayed pretty much the same for much of history. They were built from wood or metal and attached to the body with leather straps.

Around 200 B.C., Roman warrior Marcus Sergius lost his hand in battle. A special iron hand was built for him. The hand was even shaped to hold his shield. Sergius was able to fight again!

In modern times, computers and new materials help doctors make improved, high-tech artificial limbs. There are special attachments, hinges that allow for movement, and surfaces that look like real skin. But that's not all. New technology lets a person's thoughts control robotlike body parts! Your brain sends signals through nerves to your body's muscles. This causes you to move. The brain sends these signals even if the muscles aren't there anymore. But your nerves can be connected to a bionic (mechanical) body part. Brain signals make the bionic part move. How cool is that?

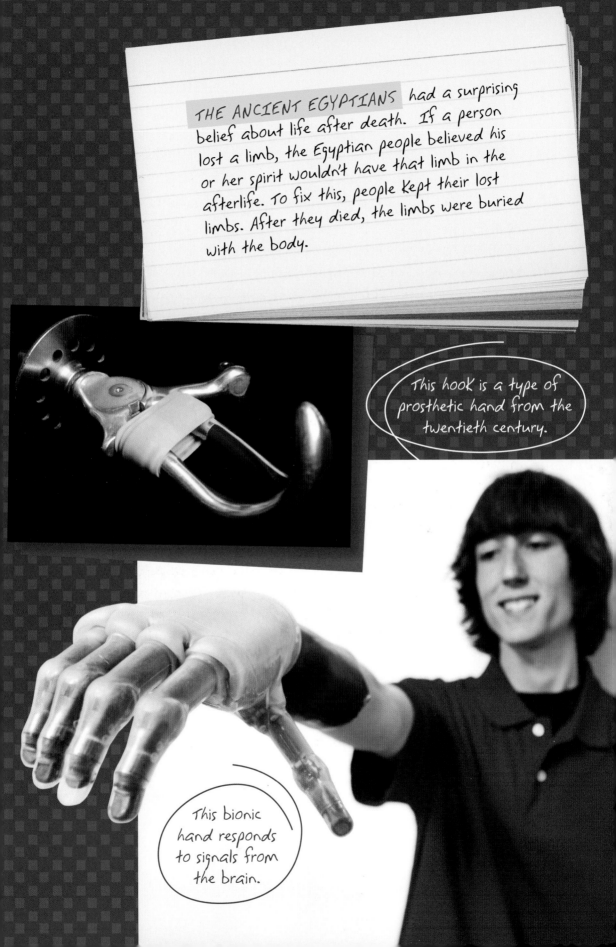

THE ANCIENT EGYPTIANS had a surprising belief about life after death. If a person lost a limb, the Egyptian people believed his or her spirit wouldn't have that limb in the afterlife. To fix this, people kept their lost limbs. After they died, the limbs were buried with the body.

This hook is a type of prosthetic hand from the twentieth century.

This bionic hand responds to signals from the brain.

GLOSSARY

abrasive: a substance used for cleaning. In toothpaste, abrasives clean away the gunk in your teeth.

artificial: false, or created by humans

atom: one of many tiny particles that make all physical things. The human body is made up of atoms.

bionic: mechanical but similar to a part of the human body

brain stem: an area of the brain that controls activities such as sleep

bristle: a short, stiff hair used on a brush. Most modern toothbrushes are made with nylon bristles.

cathode ray: a stream of particles called electrons that travels out of a heated tube

cerebral cortex: an area of the brain that is involved with the sense of touch and the feeling of pain

detergent: a substance that loosens dirt to be cleaned away. In toothpaste, detergents loosen the gunk in your teeth.

fluoride: a substance that strengthens teeth. Fluoride is found in toothpaste and in drinking water.

laser: a beam of light that shines in one direction

mercury: a metal that is liquid at ordinary temperatures and is used in thermometers

orthodontist: a dentist who specializes in changing the direction of teeth

particle: an extremely small piece

photon: a tiny particle of radiation that carries energy

radiation: a form of energy, such as light or heat, that is released by an object

spinal cord: a group of nerves located in a person's spine. The spinal cord connects the brain to other parts of the body.

x-ray: a stream of radiation that can travel through solid objects and allow doctors to capture images inside the body

FURTHER INFORMATION

Ballen, Karen Gunnison. *Seven Wonders of Medicine.* Minneapolis: Twenty-First Century Books, 2010. Take a close look at some of the most amazing things that doctors can do.

Band-Aid—Fun for Kids
http://www.band-aid.com/fun-for-kids
Try out fun activities and test your knowledge about injuries at the official Band-Aid website.

Bredeson, Carmen. *Don't Let the Barber Pull Your Teeth: Could You Survive Medieval Medicine?* Berkeley Heights, NJ: Enslow Publishers, 2012. This book gives readers a gross look at medicine during medieval times, an age before the dawn of modern medical inventions.

Ferris, Julie. *Ideas That Changed the World.* New York: DK Publishing, 2010. Check out this book for more medical inventions, as well as other important inventions throughout history.

KidsHealth—For Kids
http://kidshealth.org/kid
This fun site from KidsHealth has fact sheets, quizzes, movies, and more. The site's pages cover everything from medical terms to how the body works.

Kids Work!
http://www.knowitall.org/kidswork/hospital/index.html
This interactive site provides information about the history of medicine and what it's like to work at a modern hospital.

Rosen, Michael J., and Ben Kassoy. *Odd Medical Cures.* Minneapolis: Millbrook Press, 2014. This book focuses on the many wrong-headed and wacky ways doctors have tried to help the ill.

Royston, Angela. *Heroes of Medicine and Their Discoveries.* New York: Crabtree Publishing Company, 2011. Learn more about medical inventions and the people behind the discoveries.

Woods, Michael, and Mary B. Woods. *Ancient Medical Technology: From Herbs to Scalpels.* Minneapolis: Twenty-First Century Books, 2011. Read about the many methods ancient healers used to treat their patients.

Woog, Adam. *The Bionic Hand.* Chicago: Norwood House Press, 2010. Read all about the creation of the world's first bionic hand.

INDEX

PHOTO ACKNOWLEDGMENTS

The images in this book are used with the permission of: Illustrations by: © Laura Westlund/Independent Picture Service; © Don Farrall/Photodisc/Getty Images, p. 5 (left); © iStockphoto.com/Marilyn Barbone, p. 5 (right); © Science Source/Photo Researchers, Inc., p. 7 (inset); © Jannoon028/Dreamstime.com, p. 7; © Dave King/Dorling Kindersley/Getty Images, p. 9 (top); © Nir Alon/Alamy, p. 9 (bottom); © iStockphoto.com/High Impact Photography, p. 11 (middle); Science Museum/Wellcome Library, London, p. 11 (bottom); © iStockphoto.com/wdstock, pp. 11, (top) 13 (bottom), 25 (bottom), 29 (top); © Todd Strand/Independent Picture Service, pp. 13 (middle), 17 (bottom); © Sander Jurkiewicz/Alamy, p. 13 (top); © RMN-Grand Palais/Art Resource, NY, p. 13 (bottom/inset); © Stocksnapper/Dreamstime.com, p. 15; © iStockphoto.com/Nicholas Belton, p. 17 (top); © Lightpoet/Shutterstock.com, p. 19 (top); © Bettman/CORBIS, p. 19 (bottom); © Brad Wilson/Stone/Getty Images, p. 21 (top); © SSPL via Getty Images, p. 21 (bottom left); © BIU Sante (Paris), p. 21 (bottom right); © iStockphoto.com/Belterz, p. 23 (inset); © JGI/Jamie Grill/Blend Images/Getty Images, p. 23; © Astier/BSIP/SuperStock, p. 25 (top); © Bettmann/CORBIS, p. 25 (middle); © Keith Morris/Alamy, p. 27 (bottom); © The Print Collector/Alamy, p. 27 (top); © UIG via Getty Images, p. 29 (middle); © Barry Austin/Glow Images, p. 29 (bottom);
Front cover: iStockphoto.com/Rob McRobert.

Main body text set in Highlander ITC Std Book 13/16.
Typeface provided by International Typeface Corp.

LERNER

Expand learning beyond the printed book. Download free, complementary educational resources for this book from our website, www.lerneresource.com.

SOURCE